Not Just A Passing Cloud

Khyati Arora

Made with ❤ on the BookLeaf Publishing Platform

www.bookleafpub.in

www.bookleafpub.com

Dedication

To Hyderabad's auto-rickshaws - your incessantly
crackling engine noise (symphonies) and
(un)comfortable seats, shook these poems loose.

To my super-heroes - my parents and my sister,
you guys rock.

Preface

I spent days thinking about what to include in the
preface. Should it be a flashing warning, instructions to
store this book (cold environment, away from children,
close to sunflowers, etc.)?
But I figure I can suggest to you how to read it.

This book is braided with deliberate knotting and
looping of poems, from one thought to the next, so yes,
they are in a certain order. An intentional journey. But
there is entropy around and within us, so you can open
any page and find something to carry with you.

You might stumble into strange intersections of comfort
and mortality, moments where heartbreak is awkwardly
sandwiched between humor and dark humor. Some
poems were written with a grin, some through gritted
teeth. The poems walk a delicate tightrope between
serenity and violence. And also lean heavily into
nostalgia - achingly so.
Reader discretion is advised, hehe.

I am a genetic counselor by profession, so don't be
surprised when you see science here. Anatomy disguised
as poetry, physiology humming beneath metaphors,

emphasizing the chemistry that causes all emotions. The
body is my muse, it is the first place we live, and
sometimes the hardest place to stay.

But mostly, I hope this feels like sitting quietly with
someone who notices the same odd corners of the day as
you do. I might have made up some words, please
embrace them as you would any other, small,
misunderstood creature.

So welcome in,
make yourself comfortable,
there is tea on the side, a chair by the window,
and no wrong place or time to begin.

Acknowledgements

This book was made in secret.
The quiet kind, you keep from even yourself until it
grows too big to ignore.
However, it wouldn't exist without the small, miraculous
acts of my favorite people:
Papa, who delivered chai at precisely the right intervals,
like he'd been handed a schedule by the universe itself.
Mumma, who kneaded the tension out of my shoulders
without asking why it was there.
And my sister, whose check-ins came without context
but always at the moments I needed to remember that
someone, somewhere, was looking out for me.

Thank you to **BookLeaf Publications** for making the idea
of writing a book feel not just possible, but inevitable.
For championing people like me, who only dreamed of
having a book to their name.

To every person who turns these pages—
Whether you've read one poem, three lines, or just
opened it to see the number of pages -
Thank you. You are a part of it now.
You should know you've made a dent in my little
universe just by being here.

And lastly, to the versions of me who thought these
poems would eternally remain in the draft - you're not
only nerdy and weird, but also published now :))

1. Home

when your words walk to me
i'll write a letter to tomorrow
so i can remember more of you,
home.
i look outside the window,
for a place devoid of the feelings
i have instilled over time, for you
under the light of my lamp
the same shades
and its luminescence
that I spilled over my lap
and dried under the sun,
the tears that were engraved
on the wooden floor
as scars to the beautiful, beautiful,
home.
i found people
and called them home
offering them the power to make me
homeless,

but each time I traced
the map of your coordinates
i found my way back.
i stare at the corner
where wall meets wall
where laughter lingers
you remind me to smile,
home.
thank you, you raised me well,
home.

2. Dada's home

buildings are silent stories
(pun intended)
they carve permanence
force establishment
and bonding
they give you a spot to call
community
dada spoke often of leaving
his once homeland
stitched behind him
partitioned by lines
he found a new place
just a bunch of bricks
trembling
until exile melted into
"ghar"
all corners that made him smile
sowed plants
hibiscus and tulsi
that would sing to him

his evening music
his chai
that he would at times spill
like the sunset
friday nights
of intense political conversations
and fragile treaties
debating histories
he never liked it when I chewed gum
he romanticized letters and bank work
he laughed with his eyes
and we spent most evenings
walking around
hands clasped at our backs
in discipline
and so much warmth

3. Terrace and time

yes
i imagine living in the 19th century
the frosty winters of december
pinching my wrists
and the tip of my nose
last night
i dreamt of going back there
sleeping under the stars
the mosquitoes, a quick battle
afternoons with kites flying
evenings spent jumping parapets
of neighboring terraces
cuss words noticeable only to those
from the town
peachy giggles and flirtatious stares
across the verandah
excuses only a grandmother could pardon
while pickles blistered under the sun
and chilies warned the breeze
a bed that tasted like india

the stories of old men and their chillum
that never get old
the day was worth laboring
in the anticipation of the sleep
but nature took its course
time kept its promise
now
there are buildings scratching the skies
where those kites would fly
a chasm of societal eyes
blanketing those nifty chuckles
a serious spider's web between each parapet
a little less of home
and now i come sleep in my bed

4. Bazaar

We visited a bazaar the other day. Here is something along the lines of seven degrees of reinventing a poet's stream of thought;

1. Incomplete without the screaming vendors; they weigh goods about seventy-seven times each day, but always remember to load with scarves of resilience and a stack of monetary change.

2. Spurring fragrance of the flowers; an evident testimony of the butterflies in my stomach.

3. Junk jewelry; found myself falling into a pit of oxidized jhumkas in the center of the bazaar only to be tapped back into reality, by the lilt and jolt of a Vespa.

4. Dauntless streets; Ashok, 11 years old, worked on the streets since age 5, he's a master of his business, sells chai, says phobias make you stronger, and doesn't give a damn to the big mouths.

5. Scorching heat; skin burns are only normal, they can turn your body into a wall, and well, what do you do? Paint it.

6. Walking consumes less energy currency, mostly

because you get pushed through the huddled crowd, elbow to elbow is distance enough. Besides, etiquette and hygiene are a myth, no?

7. Bargain; not a penny more than 50% of whatever you say. Haha.

Bazaars are comfortable. Malls are an effort. And air-conditioned. But that's about it. Bazaars connect me back to home. The entire Venn diagram is me trying to pick the right carrots for halwa on a December winter morning with dada, in the bazaar.

5. Colors of ordinary

when I was sixteen
i read a thesis
on the colors in Shakespeare's work
one question stayed,
"is your blue my red?"
i believe in science
this could be nothing more
than a glitch in perception
a trick of light
bent through the lens of a human mind
and yet, how poetic a thought
that we may live in the same world
but see it entirely differently

this was reason enough to pause
to celebrate the shape of my ordinary
the ordinary that shows me
muted greys on mornings
when i rise only to draw the curtains
or on other days

the soft pink on my cheeks
the green panic in the chest
when i realize i forgot to feed my fish
the yellow certainty
that today is a good day to do laundry
the ordinary
an amalgamation of
regularly occurring crests, that we call extraordinary
and the inevitable troughs that humble them
so, give yourself a moment
swallow the presence of plenty
you are lucky to call this your ordinary

6. When time left me

since I am young,
i am inevitably mistaken to be wrong
maybe I grew up
only in my mind
maybe I grew up
as a time, space, and age conspiracy
maybe I just didn't.
but I will.

since i am young,
i believe i will write a memoir
one day
reliving my art,
my joy, my arguments,
the gentle bells,
the warm cinnamon buns
times when i could see the moon
with my naked eyes
half-done to-do lists
rituals

clean linens and kitchen floors
steady things
i thought would always stay

since i am young,
i am thought to easily be
unhopeful
too early for nostalgia
too late for innocence
my age is just a number
do i belong to it?
maybe i don't
because **maybe i grew up**

7. Daisies to daggers

and you know what freedom does to people
it makes them run
straight to the sea
water up to their knees
salt clinging to our ankles
barefoot on white sand
some times
holding daisies in their pockets
other times, holding daggers
and we're all creatures of waiting
for an invisible axis to tilt
susceptible to blaming all universal energies
when things go haywire, fracture
blame all powers, but ourselves
for our own sins
and vices
the powers
never promised to stay anyway
the vagueness in our behaviors
do you ever know when

petals sharpened to steel?
yearning blurred into hunger?
do you ever know anything, for sure?
we have freedom of thought
but caged in a parabolic bowl
of age and time
and conscience
because we don't know at which point
we became
more hopeful, and less hopeless
more human, and less animal
more lucid, and less illusion

8. Sensory party, sensitive party-goer

have you ever smelled
another person's insecurity?
someone's coffee
smelled like they were afraid
the scent of
hesitation
the cup trembling in their hands
you might not savor their offering.
or, have you tasted questions?
some that we create
some that we attract
the rest that we inherit
those that they leave behind.
the heirlooms, the age-old
the ones that our traditions ask each other
whispering in each other's ears,
a safe distance from each other's backs
have you ever heard that?
the hush between words

the silence of audacity
the ghost of purpose
i might have
not pointing fingers

(i say sensory party because all my senses are always
sniffing doubt, tasting tension, and eavesdropping on the
unsaid, they're having a party :D)

9. Audition

young girl auditions for her audacity:
punishes herself with a gun pressed to her lips

said,
her parents held a casting call for a *good* daughter
said,
the insides of her brain, and stomach revolted, a quiet
insurrection
said,
she is a soul, not just a body,
not just an ornament of obedience
said,
it must rain, help her mix her grief in what must not be
known
said,
acts of attachment must confine in a space that is tender
not tremble in hesitation
so now,
she doesn't leave the windows of her room open
anymore

said,
she is a letter that reached late
she is coffee that is too sweet
she is maternity leaves that turn into resignation
but
she is also origami
she is Tan Hua flowers that blossom once
and remembered for eternity
she is a recycled plastic bottle
enduring
she knows,
she isn't mediocrity,
she is the sum of every whispered rebellion
she is a cave of wonders
she isn't lonely, she is lightening
if you don't know this, you must.
you are no different.
don't put a gun in your mouth.

it'll be before you know that
you'll be standing on your bones

10. The stains that make us; splitch-splotch

stains from the inkpot
splotch onto me
as I sign the last of the letters

stains of blood
splotch over my table linen
escaping my veins and,
blossoming a flower pattern
as i try to chop myself the last of mushrooms

stains of people
splotch over my soul
sinking
as i try to grow myself
into the person
who dances with herself
in almost-damp socks on a rainy thursday evening
who paints comic characters on her walls for halloween
cleans her shelf of books

just to find something from a long time back
maybe dried flowers
a lover's note as a bookmark
or perhaps, just a sigh of who i used to be
but most importantly,
i want to grow into someone
who makes candles for herself
now my soul - I have cleaned
scrubbed and polished
this I am certain
but i know
we're all teenagers
in the bodies of grown people.

11. COVID

all this while
we've been living in a fantasy
a mirage of permanence
a trick of time
tell me
if you ever imagined
a civil war at your porch
a zombie apocalypse in your backyard
a nuclear bomb in your balcony
or a disease slowly eating away parts of humanity
i told you, we're living in a fantasy
unpredictable
where we think we are safe
a soothing assumption
but are we?
we are.
we are.

12. Rumor

in times we lived
breathing air
freshly made for our lungs
posing for photographs
on the edge of peril
taking selfies in dangerous situations
cracking puns
at inappropriate scared times
it all seemed sublime

now

it isn't
hypocrites walking the alleys
faulting the lines of truth
between subjective and objective
an endless duel
where did we misplace that air
they say freedom is liberating
so we ascend the mountains
converse with clouds
about how to qualify

as a weather reporter
make sand castles
punch the sea foam
and carve the seaweed
i long for the ease of refusal
the privilege to say
"i'd rather stay in"
and rumor has it
the world was once locked down

13. Life of the party

as we remained chained
within the soft cages of our homes
some dared call this freedom
but
turning the news off for a hot minute
is highly recommended
there is no truce with this monster
there is only making the best out of it
whilst it walks our neighbourhood
whilst it has a gala time at the hospitals
whilst it crowns itself
the life of the party
whilst we are home
rooting ourselves
anchoring in humility
our heads in the clouds
for ambition refuses to sleep
and our feet to the ground
for each of us is certainly grateful)
a roof above

enough food to turn some into chefs
poets of our palates
enough cleaning to sculpt abs from dust
and just the right amount of family
to remind us that happiness,
though small,
multiplies when shared

outside, the monster parades
inside, we learn the art of stillness
the art to live
how ironic.

14. Me-di-o-cri-ty

who defines mediocrity?
we spend too much time
making birds from origami
humming a song instead of screaming it
tapping our feet to a tune
under the table
tactile enough to keep it secret
so no one mistakes us for wanting more
we don't write enough
for the fear it won't make sense
even to us
we spend too much time
trying to cry pretty
so tell me
who is defining mediocrity
and boxing the extraordinary
into mundane
mundane is not failure
ordinary is not an apology
it exists because it is beautiful

because we find happiness in routine
it is its own form of worship
we can romanticize anything we like
without being a prodigy at it
and you, the beloved passerby
can appreciate anyone as you please
your fish, cat, dog, horse
or yourself
and anyone next door
the unnoticed life
is never small.

15. On the brink of belief

we live in a fantasy
fooling ourselves
into untraceable faith
dwindling beliefs
swinging dogmas
pendulums of doctrine
swinging from
birthright to blasphemy
canonizing the living
forgiving the dead
rejoicing in the same places
you've put tags and titles and labels
insisting borders and confinement
so what do you do?
you siphon fragments of joy
from a source
a person
her
and well
her laughter

perforates your heart
you might worship her
make a cathedral out of her marrow
you'd kneel if she demanded
you'd believe if she said
you'd want to
you know, all people
plants
insects
even corpses
are fabulous, and flawed
they rest houses
they may draw lines on culture
for good
scribble margins around traditions
break the curfew of flags
rehearse disobedience
against the architects of violence
so tell me
you radiant conspiracy of a woman,
will God ever be able to recover from the beauty he's
given you?

16. Pretty woman

wearing a lipstick called Love Letter
draped in a saree
in the shade of midnight blue
she stood there
unwavering
by the slurs of a 2 am street
well, it could be because
she knew she was beautiful
not the kind that merely turns heads
no
she was brave
and dangerous
the kind that turns tides
the street lights dimmed in reverence
too timid to challenge her glow
for only she could be the light of the street
she's the kind people write songs about
her yawns giving hope to the morning
her laugh making you bite your tongue
hair like poetry, spilling over her shoulders

it can wrap the whole of you
her bangles weaving prayers into the wind
cycling through the narrow streets of her temple
so
keep her safe
keep this consciousness safe inside your soul
become the reason someone believes
in a world
where the night does not devour its daughters.

17. Mixtapes & Medusa

the way you carry yourself is admirable
a tempest stitched into silk
your energy so fierce
your spirit so untamed
your love so dangerous
even the chaos you call craft
im hinting to the mix tapes you made me
your words so unworried
reckless symphonies
the song of freedom
you pleading, chanting
your vehement rant on why Medusa was mistreated
"justice for medusa, hoohaa"
well, so the night came
"let's ditch this party and go to the lake"
with embellished streetlights
well, so the dawn touched
tucked between dormant spines
the library slumbers
blanketed by shelves

and bad weather
i mean good rain
and thunder
trading constellations
and pillow talk
im trying to recreate
my moments with you
won't you help me?

18. Bread

today i was reminded of
this mountain i had climbed
because today i feel like a pebble
strange
i was reminded how the peak
had a halo of clouds
and i was standing above it
like jack, the weeper
it was windy and sweaty
at the same time
it felt like the cloud had rained on my neck
so we decided to eat a sandwich
and descend
when we spotted a woodpecker
well, everyone but me
it had some ambitions
intentions that neither me
nor my sandwich
could anticipate
and there, in a twisted fate

my sandwich was in the beak of a woodpecker
flying 20ft above sea level
"mean" sea level
i was reminded today
of the essential discussions on our trek
about the anatomy of bread
and how the woodpecker
most certainly
had its own ambitions
my sandwich its small salvation
And somewhere
Between ascent and appetite
I forgave
it would not have appreciated the sandwich
as much as i would have
after all,
as Polonius said to his sons
"to thine own self, be true"
even if the truth is
stolen bread.

19. My tree

knock knock
who's there?
my love, for you
only what is left of it
there was once a tree
that grew inside of me
inside my lungs
its branches
drooping out as my hair
the sweet nectar of its fruits
flowing out of my mouth
my eyes were its butterflies
and nurtured the tree
with my own hands
dirt in my fingernails
mud in my pants
scabs on my knuckles
tears on my shoes
i grew this tree
shared some fruits with you

i also grew fear
and one day
you walked into my forest
uprooted my tree
picked your axe
and swung it like a prayer
splitting my trunk
cutting me
into slabs of wood
stacking into planks
to make a door
and now you
knock knock

20. Ruined reverence

there's a portrait of you
i have in my head
a version of you
like a personally curated playlist
or handpicked herbs from my backyard
because i know which leaf
would dissipate the exact taste
i have built you within me
like man made architecture
like man made religion
like man made constellations
a language which exists
because we allow it
syllable by aching syllable
i gave you the power
to be in my thoughts
to be a miser of my joy
to be the wonder of my day
to become my love letter
i made this version of you

that liked the way
i painted on your back
it's just unsettling
how you and i cannot co-exist
for worlds could collide
for swords have nothing on us
for you are just
a figment of my imagination
and i gave you that power to you.

21. The feast

there's a portrait of you
i have in my head
a version of you
like a personally curated playlist
or handpicked herbs from my backyard
because i know which leaf
would dissipate the exact taste
i have built you within me
like man made architecture
like man made religion
like man made constellations
a language that exists
because we allow it
syllable by aching syllable
i gave you the power
to be in my thoughts
to be a miser of my joy
to be the wonder of my day
to become my love letter
i made this version of you

that liked the way
i painted on your back
it's just unsettling
how you and i cannot co-exist
for worlds could collide
for swords have nothing on us
for you are just
a figment of my imagination
and i gave you that power to you.

22. The switch is there

i wish you could meet me now
now, that I am a better me
unfastening the rusted chains
of the past
when I'm my safe haven
in the refuge of my ribs
i'm just a beautiful battlefield
where the war has softened
into wildflowers
some nights
i cup my hands
kneeling
and pray apologies to myself
to the girl who waited for me
i deserve more than just skincare
i deserve self-care
i deserve sanctuary
and while my body
still remembers gravity
my mind has grown translucent

light tyndal-ling between thoughts
i am an easy friend now, i think
at least I hope to be
for you
so next time your positive thoughts
go bankrupt
knock on my door
let me show you the sunflowers
how they shapeshift with the light
and three stars to the left in the sky
let me read you Kafka
until the dark
feels like velvet
but
if you wish to leave
leave me to the hum
of my own becoming
if you wish to leave
please turn the light off.

23. My spot

there's a spot
i'd like to show you
here, come
hold my hand
no, don't look at my fingers
and catch up
run at my pace
don't worry about the dirt
don't worry about the moss
don't worry about the rain
don't worry
the spot is where the sun sets
only when i want it to
in the colors only i like
orange blood
purple bruises
concealed with pink care
making peace
with the blue thunderclouds
it's a spot

and i was thrilled to show it you
there's bees and birds and butterflies
dewed flowers and frozen spider webs
and sometimes it growls
like a beast
and i thought you weren't scared
so i wanted to show you the spot
but you ran out of breath
running
and now
i have to reach my spot
alone
my heart
i will come.

24. Free fall

screamed -
and silence was the only song
i sat
throwing knives in the dark
whispering to the fog above the lake
immeasurably far from the shore
tuning out
writing into my days, and my nights
exposing the tattoos etched
into my wounded skin
revealing all my influences
all the cracks fraying the edges of my pages
pages, so easily crumbled
and crushed
but souls can't
slow, I see the sky bleeding light
clouds lined with fire
orange streaks of the naked sun
night's sweet parting
patchy glimpses of what's to come

the wind carrying a quiet promise
i can smell it
my bare feet in the white warm sand
haunted by no ghosts
somehow
entropy felt safe
because every day after that day
felt like a free fall.

25. Philosophy of Digestion; don't eat feelings

i am the nucleus
in this cell of a world
sleeping in a petri dish
a harmony of sorts
or something i failed at
i am the cronchy leaves
that kids love to crush
the ones that change their color
a little faster
i am the sharpness of a knife
the steel
elegantly dicing mushrooms
and stubborn carrots
(mentioning carrots because i am emotionally attached
for inarticulable reasons)
i am a staggered confession
i am the drunk seeking attention
the one who loses their way
the one who thinks of lovers

and galaxies and politics
planning future uprisings
a monologue unraveling
so one night
i decided to end what it feels like
to be in a cell
to be the crunchy-cronchy leaves,
to be shining at edges like a knife,
to be intoxicated into another dimension,
like slapped into an out-of-body experience
so i ate them
gulping the ache
chewing the ghosts
and instantly felt something
dancing in my throat
a writhing lump
then i spat everything out
yuck
it was a nightless identity crisis
but it was catharsis
and i sat by the window
like it meant something
stomach emptied of sentiment
a philosopher in exile
with new perception

learning outcome: don't eat feelings.

26. Sacred love

go and love someone
exactly the way they are
not as the world told them to be
not as the mirror asked them to become
easier said than done
but when you do
they'll transform into a
tinted and
decorated version of themselves
you'll see them for who they are
all the quirks, rough edges,
and unresolved emotions
that will only pour out
as
love towards you
you'll see them for who they are
stained clothes, scratched specks
curled hair, frequent crying
leftover food, incomplete paintings
and love will happen

again and again
because to be accepted is
one of life's most
gentle miracles
we are by design
humans
and have the extraordinary power
of falling in love

27. The Theory of Hope

an ode, then
to the persistent hope
the hope that knocks on my door
but leaves before i open it
the hope i cultivate
watching strangers smile
at crosswalks
the hope
when old patterns loosen their grip
the hope that explanation brings
promises tucked into my mum's saree pleats
the hope that new curtains entail
the curtains that watch me
in all my hues and seasons
bruised and mended
not mistaking my survival
for weakness
i always thought i was lunar by nature
a moon child
but now someone else

breathes on those curtains
and i hope
the curtains don't look at them
the same way they looked at me
in that delicate relinquishing
i gather myself
this thought, of hope
makes me look after myself
it tells me i can count on me
steady, friendly
just the hope.

28. The rain agrees with me

we've all scraped our knees
enough to understand
what healing feels like
it's after a day
without a whiff of a breath, almost
i mean, I was in bed after all
the fan stared at me, gawking
humming
i switched it off to hear
the now powering sound of the rain
oh, how it instantly set my thoughts free
unfastening them
does this even make sense?
an assemblage of drops
on my window sill
or the wires running from pole to pole
it's not just noise
just like art is never just art
if you listen closely
even the dead seem to be breathing

soon, i realize
my heart, brady
i realize
i am content with the day I lived
the day that offered me obstacles
and reward in equilibrium
today the crevices of my back are saturated
i no longer remain a pendulum
trying to make ends meet
i''m not worried about tomorrow
and the rain outside agrees with me
i almost came back to the real world
didn't know it only showered
to become my muse.

29. Jazz

i rocked on my old chair
to some jazz beats
with a side of
toast and eggs
getting cold
wondering
if I could play good memories
on my stereo
like coming home on crowded trains
letting the world pass me by
station names blurring
feet aching
spine dancing
and i intend to hold onto that feeling
satisfaction
that elusive creature
it perches quietly on my shoulder
it is enough
that i can listen to music i like
that i can grow plants

give life
but guess what happened yesterday
i was fixing my stereo
lit a candle
summoned a warmer glow
and i smelled a burning insect
oh the grief
fire is play for a man
and I rocked on my chair
playing some jazz
and happy memories
i eloped with gratification
bye.

30. Circular hours

i learned to love early mornings
golden hour secrets
the funny shadows
absurd
as if they too, are trying to remember
who they belong to
i wake up but am not out of the bed
possibly cataloging the light
strange habits
in an age where we constantly
attempt to document our lives
our life seems a lot more circular
than linear
experiences and
learnings, always come back
nature prefers loops
the light,
it comes back to me some days
but
with every sunrise,

i learned to wake up by myself
i understand that not many people
are going to ask me how i slept
what i'm trying to say is
others company is nice
but i like mine too.

31. Love/Home/Sickness

dear family
of course
it is beyond crack of midnight
poets take time very unceremoniously
i write because i have
diagnosed myself with
lovesickness
you are my home
and so i thought it was
homesickness
but turns out
it was disguised
turns out
i can't hold myself together
when the Lumineers sang Ophelia
"heaven help the fool who falls in love"
heaven knows they referred to me
turns out
and i repeat
i am brittle

turns out
i want to lay my head on your shoulder
i want to hold your palm in mine
i want to brush my elbow to yours
while we cross paths in the kitchen
and lose my senses in the
residual fragrance of your shower gel
turns out
i want to hear you call me
"sweetie pie" and "princess"
tease you so i can savor
your precious laugh
tire you so i can devour
how you close your eyes
but turns out
there might be days
that we are more apart
and distance is just an excuse
but i will bear you in my mind
knowing i linger in yours
in my feisty pajamas
messy hair
and so
next time
when you go to sleep
please
take me with you.

32. A fourth more than half; arithmetic love

as my mom asked me for half a glass of water
i gave her a fourth more than half
because it does matter
someone, somewhere
is keeping tally
as a remembrance
not me though
because that's what I do,
i'll hold the door open for you a little longer
i'll give you the larger slice of pizza
i'll bring you unconditional cookies
and hang a little longer
in the parking basement
to make you feel safe

not all kindness is seen, just little breadcrumbs of love.

33. Sisterhood

there's comfort
in knowing
that my past self
wasn't learning to walk alone
it was bound to a soul
someone who shared
the same home
the same womb
when i was ten
she was half my age
and twice as beautiful
she surrendered her hair
to my clumsy braids
pleasured in hand-me-downs
and held the balloons i gave her
like pieces of art
so close to her face
occasionally kissing
there's comfort
in knowing

that my past self
wasn't a myth
a magician's trick
or fiction
someone saw me grow
someone who wasn't me
yet i love them more
their funny silhouettes
hugging me from across
the room we share
a fleeting glance
even when our mothers' language
rested between us
there's comfort
in knowing
that my present self
has someone
who, just as much as me
loves grocery runs.

34. Best friend

you are not
a friendship day bracelet
a "have you reached home" text
a coffee *spill-the-tea* date
an "ask your mom for a sleepover"
a meal that we shared
a sanitary napkin you sneaked for me
a color of happiness on my face
you are not these things
but you still look, expectantly
outside your window
if i stand holding a jukebox
playing *our song* from grade eight
and i say this because
people lose friends to distance
to jealousy of new companionship
to a chasm of
when you wanted to cry
and share about how tough work is
but not when you made latte art

or when you had a good hair day
because
feelings and time get in the way
suddenly double texting your bff
becomes embarrassing
thinking if they will ever
share their clothes with you again
it becomes uncomfortable
because
when you are away from home
everything
everything seems far away
and you look at the picture
of you and your best friend
that you safely taped from the edge
on your cupboard
because
someday they will ask you
"how was your day?"
and it would feel the exact same
from five years ago.

35. Yellow

i wore a yellow hat
everyday
in the rattling bus
so whenever people saw me
they laughed
and i laughed back
they looked at me
like i made them happy
because when Richard Siken said
"everyone i know is in some kind of pain"
he was the opposite of inaccurate
so when they saw the sun
her aura like flowers
a girl with a yellow hat
an omen of ease
blowing warm air into her palms
they knew they could smile
because her eyes birthed moons
you have nothing to fear in this life

the world is an intimate place to live
and you can smile.

36. Pangaea

i like to create
it anchors me
in the cradled gravity of sentiment
as if some mystical hand
once gathered the shards of earth
pressed them together
then broke them apart
splitting them
Like pangaea or something
this maximally
translates into
how i experience spaces
how i taste truth
how i dance under water
my pupils dilating at the colors
a kaleidoscope
beyond the language of my
mediocrity
marveling at ephemeral life
tender nostalgia like abstract art

and somehow
going back to my ink
until next morning.

37. My painting

i hurriedly dressed
ignoring the unlawful pleasures
incomplete touches
the marks it would've left
on my duvet
all without a quiver
we unfolded separately
from artful streaks
to the breathless chuckles
of how it made me feel
oh, so wonderful
we were late, we walked on the street,
uneasy, clumsy
a mischievous dance of steps.

i speak of no man or woman
but my painting
the one I adorned in my dreams
in moonlight
holding it in my palms

with my brown curly hair
bound with a paintbrush
people suspect
my pulse rising on the street.
i feel their suspicion walking with me
a twin shadow
i hear their disbelief in art
i don't let my tears blur the streetlights
i go faster
daring them to think

but what greater wealth to an artist than this?
what I create today has already been birthed in my past
and my muses today are my art tomorrow.

38. *Poof*

what would i do if poetry vanished?
what would i do
if my muse laced her boots
to take a walk
and never returned
what would i do if i broke my glasses?
crushed them
under the weight of what i witnessed
the trial of a crow
the unknown where-aboutery of water
what would i do
knowing that i will age
loose skin on my hands
doors seeming larger than they are
sugar crystals sweeter than they are
pages of a book, more immortal than they are
what would i do
if not investigating true crime
and serial killers
monarchs gilded in delusion

patriarchy that bejeweled women
temples that sneer
fountains that mock
mossy chandeliers
and
what would i do if poetry vanished?
i would write about it.

39. Pen//Sword
(you know the analogy)

"So you want to be a writer?"
i was caught off guard
the question slowly creeping into my senses
like ink seeping into parchment
yes, I want to be a writer
but
how could the proud world stay silent about this?
so it pointed all fingers
covered in black judgment
and scoffed, "Merely a writer"
and now,
i'm merely a writer,
How ridiculous, how naive
because everything bursts out of me
like storms swallowed whole
my patience roars when it's calm and
the libraries of the world flirt with my solitude
and yet, I am still merely a writer,
such a loser,

don't you let this out of your mind,
let it gnaw at my spine
hunching over a typewriter,
with the power to
sweep the sweet earth
below your supple-skinned feet
to write poetry that'll move even cadavers
if I'd say, the stars would shine brighter
and you'll lose faith in all that you call madness
pen is hella mightier than a sword
and I am a writer,
so mote be the peace.

40. A poem about Art

i keep searching
for subtle scenarios
to write poetry on
keep forgetting the tiny things
moments and unnoticed details
that when summed up
and piled on a potter's wheel
mixed with drops of water
become art
art that is subjective
ancient as the first flicker of fire
yet has evolved since the inception of earth
and genesis of the human mind

i am grateful for the artists
that I am surrounded with
redefining centuries
emoting what any language lacks
and
pouring color, sound, and form

to the wordless
in the run
recalibrating their own universe
because after all
art does that.